Arthur H. Porter

Historical Sketch of Niagara

From 1678 to 1876

Arthur H. Porter

Historical Sketch of Niagara
From 1678 to 1876

ISBN/EAN: 9783743443105

Manufactured in Europe, USA, Canada, Australia, Japa

Cover: Foto ©ninafisch / pixelio.de

Manufactured and distributed by brebook publishing software
(www.brebook.com)

Arthur H. Porter

Historical Sketch of Niagara

HISTORICAL SKETCH

OF

NIAGARA,

FROM 1678 TO 1876.

MAP OF NIAGARA FALLS AND VICINITY IN 1805.

Augustus Porter's House.
BUILT IN 1806, BURNED IN 1813, REBUILT IN 1818.

Steadman House.
BUILT IN 1761 BURNED IN 1813.

Fort Schlosser.

Fort Little Niagara.

A	Fort Little Niagara.	H	Old French Saw Mill.	
B	Fort Schlosser.	I	Old Stockade.	
C	Steadman House.	J K	River Road.	
D	Small Dwelling.	L	Path to the Falls.	
E P	Garden and Orchard.	O	Old Burying Ground.	
G	Old French Landing.	P P	Portage Roads.	

Falls

Grass Island

Spring

Steadman House.

BUILT IN 1761   BURNED IN 1813.

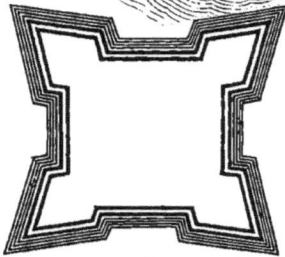

Swamp

Gill Creek

D

B   A

Fort Little Niagara.

HISTORICAL SKETCH

OF

NIAGARA,

FROM 1678 TO 1876.

NIAGARA: PAST AND PRESENT.

T HE Cataract of Niagara is one of the great natural won-
ders of the world. The name is of Indian origin, written
by the English, Iagara, Oniagara, and in more than thirty other
forms, but finally Niagara, the same first used by Hennepin, and
pronounced by the Iroquois Nyàgarah. Its signification is not
settled, but probably means nothing more than great or high
fall. This name was from the first applied by the French to
the Cataract and River, and to the Fort at the mouth of the
river. In latter times, the appellation has been extended to the
American town, near the Falls, and to the Canadian town,
opposite the Fort. In foreign countries it is only associated
with the great Cataract, and persons from the lake regions
travelling abroad, make use of it as a convenient geographical
point, to describe to foreigners the situation of places of importance at home, but comparatively little known beyond our
own country.

The Niagara River and the country adjoining, have a long
and interesting history, connected with the early French and
subsequent English occupations. A full and authentic history
of this locality can only be written after thorough research among
the early French and English colonial documents, and a careful discrimination in the use of current traditions. The interest of the subject well deserves the time and labor required to
do it justice.

In the meantime, sketches of more recent events, falling
within the personal knowledge of the narrator, or derived
from undoubted authority, may be profitably contributed as
material for future use.

A residence of more than sixty years by the narrator, and a much longer acquaintance of his father with all Western New York, and especially with this part of it, enables him to speak, with a degree of confidence, of matters of interest, some of which have become indistinct and confused in the public mind.

The broad region bordering on the St. Lawrence and the Lakes, has been the theater of great events, from the early commencement of French occupation, to the close of the last war with England. A brief reference to its early history is necessary, to a proper understanding of the importance always attached to the possession of this commanding point.

The River St. Lawrence and the Lakes formed the great waterway by which the French advanced to the Ohio and Mississippi, and acquired by means of settlements and military posts, planted along their borders, the influence and power long exercised over the Indian tribes. The possession of this channel of communication with the interior, was to decide the question of sovereignty in America between France and England. In this long chain of water communication, the Niagara River was an important link. It was the gateway to the regions beyond, and an important crossing place between the lakes. Fort Niagara commanded the passage, and as a military post ranked next in importance to Quebec.

Over all the vast regions along the lakes and beyond the Alleganies, France, by virtue of discovery and partial occupation, claimed and exercised for a very long time undisputed authority.

The history of the St. Lawrence and lake regions may be properly divided into three distinctly marked periods. The first, and longest, embraces French discovery and colonization, to the conquest and final surrender of Canada. The second, the Pontiac war and the war of the Revolution, and a few years subsequent of comparative quiet and of no special interest. The third period commences with the sale and settlement of lands purchased of the Indians, known as the Genesee Country and the Northwestern Territory. This period extends from 1788 to 1876, and within that short period of national life, the country watered by the St. Lawrence and the Lakes has made an advance in population, and in every department of material improvement, unequaled, so far as we know, in the same time in any part of the world. In 1535, more than 70 years before the English settlement at Jamestown, or the Dutch occupation of Manhattan, and eighty-five years before the landing of the Pilgrims, Jacques Cartier, the distinguished French navigator, first entered the Gulf and ascended the River St. Lawrence, called by the natives Hochelaga, to an Indian settlement of the same name, situated on the site of the present city of Montreal. On the site of Quebec he built a small fort of palisades, where he moored his vessels, and with his little band of hardy adventurers, bravely endured the rigors of a Canadian winter, and through sickness and suffering narrowly escaped utter ex-termination. On the opening of navigation, they returned to France. For various reasons the enterprise was not renewed until 1541, when Cartier again sailed for Canada, with a motley company of adventurers, in five small vessels. No better success attended his second effort for colonization. An expedition of similar character under Roberval, intended to co-operate with Cartier, was also a failure. Every attempt at permanent settle-ment, to the close of that century, shared a like fate.

In 1603, Champlain following the line of Cartier's discoveries, laid the foundation for the future growth and greatness of French influence in America. He is known as the founder of French settlements, the enterprising discoverer of new regions, and the brave defender of French rights. He is represented as a man of strong mind and sound judgment, of untiring perseverance and heroic courage.

In his first expedition in 1603, he obtained valuable informa-tion of the character of the native population, and of the geography of the country, with rude plans of the lakes, rivers and rapids, and of the great Cataract. His second expedition, in 1608, had for its objects, discovery, permanent settlement and conversion of the Indians—-by means not altogether peaceful— and the extension of French influence and power, and he engaged in his great work with a zeal and courage truly wonderful.

In 1609, he conducted an expedition of his Indian allies, against the common enemy, the Iroquois, over the lake which still bears his name.

In 1615, he ascended the Ottawa, and passing through Lake Nipissing, was the first to discover Lake Huron. Returning by a more direct course to Lake Ontario, he led a hostle expedition of the Hurons across that lake, into the heart of the Iroquois confederacy. His own discoveries, and knowledge obtained from various sources, enabled him to prepare a map, which was published in 1632, showing all that was then known of the lake regions. That map indicates correctly the position of the Falls of Niagara, but Lake Erie is scarcely recognizable; and the connection between Lakes Ontario and Huron is mere conjecture—and well it might be, previous communication with the upper lakes having been by the Northern route, by the Ottawa and Lake Huron, and so continued to be, for many years afterwards.

From 1669, under the administration of Courcelles, Talon and Frontenac, more extended plans were adopted for discoveries in the far West, of which the imperfect knowledge, derived from the Indians, had served to awaken curiosity.

Men were found and commissioned for these difficult and dangerous labors, well qualified to perform them. The names of Marquette and Joliett, the discoverers of the Mississippi, and of La Salle, the discoverer of still more remote regions, are famous in the history of the West, and will ever be remembered with admiration for their enterprise, perseverance and courage, and with respect for their religious zeal.

La Salle was especially distinguished for every qualification necessary to success. He possessed in a high degree, intelligence, sound judgment, courage, perseverance, and a vigorous constitution, with the additional advantage of influential friends, and pecuniary resources of his own, and he entered on his work with high hopes and strong confidence. In 1669, La Salle embarked on Lake Ontario for his first voyage of discovery, and under Indian guidance reached the settlements of the Senecas on Genesee River, with the hope that he might there find a guide and safe conduct to the river now known as the Ohio, of which the Indians had given information, but which had never been visited by the French. For a time he was delayed and disappointed, though not discouraged. With untiring energy and perseverance, he finally accomplished his object, and established an unquestionable claim to the discovery of the Ohio, which he descended to the falls at Louisville.

The history of Niagara and its vicinity dates from 1678, when La Salle set out on his second expedition, undertaken on high authority, with more extended views and a more liberal outfit.

The expedition, though approved by royal authority, was fitted out and sustained at the private expense of La Salle and his friends. Among his associates were Henri de Tonty, who proved a most efficient and worthy assistant, and Father Hennepin, a name familiarly associated with this locality, as the first to visit and describe the Falls of Niagara.

Embarking at Frontenac in two small vessels, they sailed directly for the mouth of Niagara River, where it was proposed to erect a small military defensive work, and with means duly provided, to construct a vessel on the river, above the Falls, in which to continue their voyage to the upper lakes.

La Salle fully comprehended the importance of the position, in connection with his plan of operations, and after some negotiations with the Indians, constructed a fort of palisades, on the site of the present Fort Niagara.

Hennepin, with others, visited the Falls, and has furnished the first description and view of the great Cataract.

His description greatly exaggerates the height, and is in other respects faulty, but the view indicates perhaps no greater changes than might be expected from a cause so constant and powerful, in a period of two hundred years. During the winter of 1678 and '9, the required vessel was built at the mouth of Cayuga Creek, five miles above the Falls, and named the Griffin. In the summer of 1679, La Salle embarked with his followers on his voyage to the upper lakes. The little vessel reached safely the trading post and Jesuit station at Mackinaw, and thence proceeded to Green Bay. From that point the Griffin, with a cargo of furs, set out on her return to Niagara, but failed to reach her destination, and was never afterwards heard from.

La Salle and his company embarked in canoes, and coasted southward along Lake Michigan to the mouth of the St. Joseph, and up that stream and across to the headwaters of the Kankakee, and descended that river and the Illinois to Peoria, near which he erected a small fort, for winter quarters and for protection against the Indians. The loss of the Griffin, and the consequent failure of expected supplies, rendered further progress impossible, and made it necessary to return to Frontenac for a new outfit. Accordingly leaving the larger part of his force to hold the fort. he set out on his long and perilous journey through snow and ice and floods, and through forests haunted by wild beasts and wily and hostile savages. But he bravely triumphed over all difficulties and dangers, and the object of his journey having been accomplished, with unabated zeal and energy, set out anew on his perilous and laborious enterprise down the Illinois to the Mississippi. Though not the first to discover, he has the distinguished honor of having been the leader of the first expedition to navigate the great river, from the interior to the Gulf of Mexico. That point being reached, he assembled his followers on the shore of the river, in view of the Gulf, and with due religious and military ceremonies, then and there, according to the custom observed by European discoverers of that day, took formal possession, in the name of his sovereign, Louis 14th, of the vast regions watered by the Mississippi and its tributaries.

His third and last expedition by sea, for further exploration and occupation, was unfortunate, but his wearisome wanderings over the same wild regions, still further connect his name and fame with the great discoveries he had made, and give him place with the most distinguished discoverers of any age. He finally died by the hand of an assassin, in the wilds of Texas, a martyr in the cause to which he had devoted his life. We honor his memory, and have good cause of satisfaction that our history commences with so worthy a name.

France from the beginning manifested great military sagacity in the selection of commanding points, and great tact in her Indian policy. Had she given more attention to permanent settlement and encouraged emigration, with the wisdom that characterized her military and Indian policy, her possession would have been more permanent, and her final overthrow more doubtful and difficult. Her military posts were judiciously chosen, and bravely maintained, and aided by her Jesuit Missionaries, and enterprising fur traders, she acquired a powerful influence over the Indian tribes. The French system was essentially military, and relied on the mother country for support, and when that failed, all was lost. This view will appear the more striking, when we remember that France preceded England in planting colonies in America, and possessing equal resources, might with a better system of colonization, have attained equal or even greater success, corresponding with the vast territory, so early and widely possessed, and so bravely defended. As late as 1757, France held all the strategic points on the line of her territorial claims. Louisburg, Quebec and Montreal, Ticonderoga, Crown Point, Frontenac, (Oswego had been captured and destroyed), Niagara,

Detroit and Mackinaw, and numerous less important posts, commanding the communication between the lakes and the Ohio and the Mississippi, with a controlling influence over all the Western tribes. At that date the English Colonies were in fact bounded on the west by the Alleganies, and the possessions of the Iroquois. But they had become impatient of restraint, and conscious of their power, the inevitable struggle for mastery, could no longer be delayed. The war was to be a bloody and decisive one, and preparations were made proportioned to the importance of the result. France put forth her best efforts for defence, and England, under the administration of Pitt, for the first time, extended liberal and powerful support to the Colonies, for the overthrow of a power, hostile to their security and future extension. Under these circumstances the result was what might have been expected. The campaign of 1758 resulted in the capture of Louisburg, Duquesne and Frontenac. That of 1759 was equally successful against Quebec, Ticonderoga, Crown Point and Niagara. And the surrender in the following year of Montreal, Presque Isle, Sandusky, Miami, Detroit and Mackinaw, and other less important posts, completed the conquest, and left England without a rival in America, and secured to the Colonies the power of indefinite extension.

The fort at Niagara occupied a position of much importance in relation to free communication westward, and as a check on the unfriendly Iroquois, and was maintained, enlarged and strengthened from time to time.

DeNonville at the conclusion of his campaign against the Iroquois in 1687, proceeded to Niagara, and erected more substantial defences. In 1725, the English threatening to establish a post at Oswego, the French saw the necessity of still further strengthening the works at Niagara. The Indians consented to the improvement at first, with the understanding that it should not be a stone fort—at a subsequent council, they waived this restriction, and the French immediately commenced the construction of the Mess house, and other substantial stone buildings, still standing. In 1755, the commencement of the French war, Niagara is represented on French authority, as in a dilapidated condition, and incapable of defence against a formidable attack. In the following year, Capt. Pouchot, an engineer of ability, employed a large force in enlarging, improving and strengthening the works, and cannon captured at Braddock's defeat, and others by Montcalm at Oswego, were added to its means of defence.

The campaign of 1759 was an eventful one, and on the part of the English and Colonial troops, eminently successful. The capture of Niagara was one of the great objects in view. The army intended for this purpose, was composed of regular and Colonial troops numbering about 2,300, with Indian auxiliaries under Sir Wm. Johnson, numbering about 1,000, the whole under the command of General Prideaux. The army embarked at Oswego on the 1st of July, and on the 6th landed at Four Mile Creek, without opposition, and proceeded immediately to invest the fort, then garrisoned by five or six hundred men, under the command of Captain Pouchot. Orders were promptly dispatched by him to the western posts for re-enforcements, and a force represented at about 600 troops and about 1,000 Indians, under Lignery and Aubry, was collected at Presque Isle, and embarked for Niagara.

Chabert Joncaire, son of Joncaire, hereafter mentioned, who was in command of the fort called Little Niagara, situated about one and a half miles above the Falls, was ordered, in case he saw any traces of the enemy, to cross the river and fall back on Niagara. Aubry and Lignery were informed of the strength and position of the enemy, and in case they did not feel able to meet them, were ordered to pass down on the west side of the river. If this order had been obeyed, the result might have been much less disastrous to the French. Although the English had a considerable force on the west side, with a battery operating against the Fort, the superiority of the French might at least have given them a temporary success, and opened communication with the Fort.

The English pressed the siege vigorously. Gen. Prideaux was killed, and the command devolved on Sir Wm. Johnson. In the meantime, the Indians had become impatient of delay, and being poorly supplied, and wavering in their attachment to the English cause, they made loud complaints and threatened to return home. Sir Wm. Johnson, with his usual tact, induced them to agree to remain for a few days, with the promise to give them the pillage of the fort, which he assured them he was nearly ready to assault. The British commander being duly informed of the approach of the enemy, made the best disposition possible of his forces to receive them. The Indians were sent forward and placed in ambush, to commence an attack on the flanks, while a force of about 700 British and Colonial troops, protected by a breastwork of trees thrown across the road, awaited the approach of the enemy in front. A bloody battle ensued, in which the French suffered a total defeat. The slaughter is represented to have been very great, and the pursuit long continued. The French troops that escaped, fled to Little Niagara, where their bateaux had been left under a strong guard, where they embarked and proceeded to Detroit. Captain Pouchot, the commander of the post, had good reason to complain that his orders for the advance on the west side of the river of the relieving force, had been disregarded, and that he had received no notice of its near approach, to enable him to render effectual assistance from the fort. He attempted to make a sortie with 150 men, but it was too late—the British were returning in force to the trenches, and he was obliged to withdraw. Pouchot makes the following statement of the condition of the garrison. One hundred and nine men had been killed and wounded, thirty-seven were sick, and the remaining four hundred were greatly reduced by fatigue—no more than

150 muskets were fit for service, the heavy cannon balls all spent, and the works injured beyond the possibility of repair or defence against a force so formidable. All hope of relief having failed, the garrison surrendered on the 25th of July, the day after the battle.

In 1719, Chabert Joncaire, a lieutenant in the French service, who had once been a prisoner with the Senecas, and adopted into their tribe—by which he obtained an influence with them, which he retained after his release—with the approbation of the Governor of Canada, applied to the Senecas, and, in consideration of his adoption, obtained from them permission to build a hut or wigwam at the lower landing of the portage. Under this license, he erected a building thirty by forty feet, surrounded by palisades, on the lower river bank at Lewiston, serving as a protection to the landing, and a place of trade with the Indians. In 1721, the English applied to the Senecas for a like privilege, which being denied, they made an unsuccessful attempt to break up Joncaire's establishment. As evidence of the importance attached by the English to the Indian trade, Gov. Burnet, in 1724, ordered Capt. Peter Schuyler to accompany an expedition of young men to settle in the Seneca country, to trade with the Indians from the upper lakes, stating that it was of great interest to the English to have a settlement on the nearest point to Lake Erie, near the Falls of Niagara, and authorizing him to purchase in His Majesty's name of the Senecas all the lands above the Falls of Niagara that they might be willing to sell, to the distance of fifty miles southward of said Falls. Although nothing resulted from this order, it shows the importance attached to the possession of this point. During all the period of French occupation, most of the supplies for the military posts and trading stations, and the furs and skins purchased of the western Indians, were transported over the portage on the backs of Indians, excepting very heavy and bulky articles, which were moved up and down the mountain by means of an inclined plane, on the most direct course to the landing, the remains of which were to be seen early in the present century.

Professor Kalm, a Swedish naturalist, on a scientific tour in America, visited Niagara in 1750. He says he found Joncaire at the carrying-place, and a settlement there of about 200 Senecas, who were employed in carrying on their backs over the portage, packs of bear and deer skins, at 20 cents a pack.

In 1757, the Indians complained to the French Governor that carts and teams were employed in transportation across the portage, in violation of their long enjoyed rights and privileges. The first landing place in use above the Falls, was at a point still known as the French Landing, about eighty rods above the rapids. LaHontan and his party going westward in 1688, transported their canoes over the portage to that place, and made a hasty visit to the Falls, which he represents as only five hundred paces distant. Through fear of the Indians he hurried back to his boats.

In 1721, Charlevoix speaks of the trading house of Joncaire at the lower landing, as before described, and also of the upper landing, which he says is about half a mile above the Falls.

Fort Little Niagara was built in 1750 on the bank of the river about one and a half miles above the Falls. It was a wooden work surrounded with palisades, with ditches and angles in the usual form. For some time it was an important Indian trading station under Joncaire, who acted in the double capacity of Indian trader, and commander of the post. It was burned and abandoned by the French during the siege of Fort Niagara. The outlines are still distinct.

In 1762, the English built another fort of similar character, about forty rods further down the river, called Fort Schlosser.

In 1806, three or four of the block houses and part of the palisades around the fort, and the dock at the landing place, were standing, and remained until destroyed in the war of 1812. The outlines can be still distinctly traced.

After the surrender of Fort Niagara, Sir Wm. Johnson and a number of his officers made a visit to the Falls with an escort of four companies of infantry.

In 1760, Major Rogers with about 200 troops set out from Niagara to receive and occupy the western posts, still occupied by the French, subject to the terms of surrender. This force embarked in bateaux at the upper landing, and proceeded on its voyage up Lake Erie, without accident or opposition, and successfully accomplished the duty assigned it.

The years of 1761 and '2 were free from any serious Indian disturbances, though unfriendly feelings, and a growing discontent under English authority, became more and more apparent. Sir Wm. Johnson, superintendent of Indian affairs, visited Niagara and Detroit in 1761, and spent a considerable time at Fort Niagara, and in the vicinity of the Falls. There could have been no fort or other building at the upper landing at that time, as he states in his journal, that he quartered in a tent. At the same time he says, men were at work on a large house for a company of Indian traders, who had been permitted by Sir Jeffrey Amherst to establish themselves at that place, enjoying a monopoly of transportation, and Indian trade. Complaints were made against this monopoly, to the English Board of Trade, by other persons engaged in the Indian trade, and by Sir Wm. Johnson, and the special privileges revoked. The large house referred to was undoubtedly that afterwards occupied by John and Philip Steadman. The current tradition is, that the same building was first erected at Fort Niagara, and used by the French as a chapel, and was afterwards taken down and rebuilt at the place named. This is rendered quite probable from the fact, that a chapel was standing in the fort in 1757, which disappeared and was never otherwise accounted for, and also that on the building occupied by Steadman—presumed to be the same—there was a steeple or belfry, an appendage not likely to have been added, unless as a part of the original building.

Furthermore on a map made by George Dember, an engineer in the British service in 1761, the whole course of the river is represented, showing the upper and lower landings, and the portage road, correctly traced, and the house referred to, placed as nearly as possible in its true position, where the old stone chimney now stands. It is not probable that the French ever erected any building on that site, or at any point, outside of their fort. Sir Wm. Johnson visited Navy Island, where two vessels were being built, one of which was nearly completed, which on his return from Detroit he met at Black Rock, laden with supplies for the western posts and trading stations. Both these vessels, a sloop and schooner, rendered important service during the siege of Detroit in 1763.

Two sunken wrecks at Burnt Ship Creek, near the lower end of Grand Island, are believed to have been French vessels, burnt after the abandonment of Little Niagara. Though there seems to be a lack of historical evidence on the subject, there is ground to believe that the French lost vessels, not otherwise accounted for, and that these hulks are the remains.[2] Sir Wm. Johnson states that an English vessel was burnt near that place in 1767.

With the close of the French war new hopes dawned on the English Colonies, of future peace and the power of unlimited extension. But great trials and sufferings were yet to be endured. The Indian power was still formidable and active, and the great Revolutionary struggle was not far distant. Though France had made a formal surrender of the long disputed territory, still French hostility and intrigue were active in stirring up the Indians to constant opposition and strife with their new masters.

In the spring of 1763, Pontiac, the celebrated Ottawa chief, had succeeded in securing the co-operation of all the western tribes in a general Indian war, to open with a sudden and simultaneous attack on all the western military posts. Mackinaw, Sandusky, Miami, Presque Isle, Le Beouf and Venango, were captured and destroyed, and their garrisons murdered or reserved for future cruelty. Detroit and Fort Pitt were invested for several months, and only saved from capture by heroic valor, through much suffering and blood. The frontier settlements of Pennsylvania and Virginia were invaded, and men, women and children murdered, or doomed to captivity and cruelty, worse than death itself.

Great exertions were made during the season of navigation to send supplies and reinforcements for the relief of Detroit. In May, Lieut. Cuyler embarked in five bateaux at Fort Schlosser with about one hundred men and supplies of ammunition and provisions. Landing near the mouth of Detroit river, they were attacked by Indians, three of the boats captured, and more than half the men killed, or taken prisoners, and afterwards cruelly tortured and put to death, Lieut. Cuyler with the remainder escaping in two boats, and returning to Niagara. Soon after, a vessel reached Detroit with about sixty men and supplies for the suffering garrison.

In July, Capt. Dalzell with 280 men and ammunition and provisions, after a long voyage in bateaux from Niagara, arrived safely at Detroit. Still the siege continued, with serious losses to the English, and the necessity for further aid was very urgent. While new forces were collecting, and needful supplies for the expedition and for Detroit were being transported over the portage of Niagara, the disastrous and bloody affair at the Devil's Hole occurred. This was an attack by a band of Seneca Indians led by the Seneca chief, Farmer's Brother, on a train of wagons, ox teams, pack-horses and attendants, with an escort of an officer and 24 men, on their way upward over the portage. The Indians lying in ambush, attacked the party by surprise, with such fatal effect that but two or three persons escaped. John Steadman, the conductor of the train, being well mounted, succeeded in making his way to Fort Schlosser. The wagons and property were destroyed, and all the cattle killed or driven away. An alarm was given to a small force of British and Colonial troops, lying at the time near Lewiston, who marched promptly to the scene of action. The Indians, aware of this movement, advanced, and again, by a like device, surprised and utterly routed them, with heavy loss. As soon as intelligence of the disaster reached Niagara, a large force was sent forward, but the Indians had all fled, and death and desolation covered the scene. Sir Wm. Johnson in an official letter says, five officers and sixty-four privates were killed and eight or nine wounded. He also expresses a fear that the loss of cattle, and the means of transportation over the portage, at so late a period in the season—the middle of September—would render it impossible to afford relief to Detroit; and we shall see that he had sufficient cause for fear. The expedition for Detroit before referred to, consisted of six hundred men with necessary supplies, under the command of Major Wilkins. For the reasons given, it was not in readiness to embark at Fort Schlosser until late in October. The Indians were on the alert, prepared for an attack, at the most exposed point in the river, described in one of the published reports of the time, as "at the east end of Lake Erie," and another as "at the entrance of Lake Erie, eighteen miles from Fort Schlosser," —at Black Rock rapids. At that point the depth of water and the rapidity of the current rendered it necessary for the boats to hug the shore, and the movement was of course slow and difficult. The attack was made on the two sternmost boats, the others being half a mile in advance, and serious loss was inflicted before assistance could be afforded and the Indians driven from their position. The loss amounted in killed and wounded to twenty-six men and three officers. The officers, and probably all the wounded men, were sent back to Fort Schlosser, and from thence to the hospital at Fort Niagara, where Lieut. Johnson died of his wounds. The return of a boat, with the wounded and the necessary guard, affords a reasonable explanation of a statement since made, that a part of the expedition was obliged to return to Fort Schlosser.

It was the 1st of November, the season of storms, when this fleet of bateaux—unfit for lake navigation at any season—set out on its voyage up the lake. When near the mouth of the Cayahoga River, these frail vessels encountered a violent storm, in which twenty bateaux were wrecked, seventy men drowned, and artillery, with ammunition and provisions in large quantities lost. Thereupon the expedition, unable to proceed, made its way back, as best it could, to Niagara.

Fortunately for Detroit, the Indians had raised the siege, and dispersed to their hunting grounds, before the fatal disaster overtook the expedition—known by the Indians to be approaching—otherwise the result might have been very different, and the worst fears expressed by Sir Wm. Johnson realized.

The Indian war had become a very serious matter, and could only be brought to a conclusion by energetic measures and a large military force. In the winter following, and preparatory to opening the campaign of 1764, Sir Wm. Johnson gave notice to all the Indian tribes, of the preparations that were making for prosecuting the war, and urged all who desired peace and the friendship of the English, to meet him in council, at Niagara in the spring. In the meantime two considerable armies were preparing for the campaign, one to advance from Fort Pitt along the Ohio, the other by way of Niagara to the country along the lakes. The latter reached Niagara early in July, under the command of Col. Bradstreet, favorably known for his success with the expedition against Fort Frontenac in 1758.

In the Indian council appointed by Sir Wm. Johnson most of the tribes were fully represented, and a great number, estimated at two thousand, besides women and children, encamped on the plain around Niagara. At first the Senecas refused to appear, but a threat to destroy their villages, brought them to terms. In due time a delegation appeared, bringing in, as required, a number of prisoners and deserters. A treaty of peace was concluded, and also a cession of land, which Sir Wm. Johnson describes as follows, in a despatch to the Earl of Halifax, dated August 30, 1764—"Your Lordship will observe by the treaty of peace with the Senecas, that they have given up all the lands from Lake Ontario to Lake Erie, of the breadth of four miles, on each side of the strait. The carrying-place is comprehended therein, and there are at present several little posts erected for its better security. They do not chose that it should become private property, as their hunting grounds are adjacent to it, but it may turn to very great use to all the posts on the communication, which is the most important of any I am acquainted with. At the time of making this cession, as your Lordship will see in the treaty, the Senecas gave me all the islands lying in the strait between the two lakes."

The cession of the islands to Sir Wm. Johnson, he says he accepted, that he might transfer them to the Crown. But he probably could not have held them, as an order in council had been issued, dated the 7th of October, 1763, "enjoining that no private person presume to make any purchase of lands, reserved to the Indians. But that if at any time, the Indians shall be inclined to dispose of any lands, the same shall be purchased only in the name and for the use of the King, at a public meeting or assembly of the Indians, held for that purpose."

Notwithstanding the treaties concluded with the Indians at Niagara, there was still need of the army at the West. But the great number of Indians in the vicinity, rendered it unsafe for Bradstreet to go forward, until their departure. In the meantime, to render his communication safe, several small stockade-posts were built along the portage, at distances of a mile apart and the outlines of several of them remained until obliterated by frequent plowing. One still remains well defined, about a mile from Fort Schlosser. A small fort was built at the same time just above the Black Rock rapids, and below the ruins of Fort Erie, for the protection of vessels, and as stated, for the convenience of laying them up in the winter.

Early in August, Bradstreet with about fifteen hundred troops, and a few hundred Indians, embarked at Fort Schlosser in a large number of bateaux, and coasted slowly along the lake, spending much time at Sandusky on useless negotiations, encouraged by the Indians merely to gain time and avoid deserved punishment, but without any decisive action. The conduct of Bradstreet was severely censured by the commander-in-chief for lack of energy in failing to chastise the Indians, as he had abundant power to have done. Still the display of so large a force, the relief of Detroit, and the re-establishment of the abandoned posts, had doubtless an important effect in dissolving the Indian league and restoring peace.

Pontiac continued irreconcilable and hostile, but his power was broken, and with it the last hope of successful resistance to English supremacy. On the return of the expedition after leaving Sandusky, it was overtaken by a violent storm, which resulted in the loss of twenty-five bateaux, most of the ammunition and baggage, together with a field train of six pieces of brass cannon. In consequence of the loss of boats, about 150 Colonial troops, under the command of Major Israel Putnam, afterwards known as General Putnam, were left to make their way through the wilderness, with great labor, and much suffering from cold and hunger, to Niagara.

Col. Bouquet, the commander of the southern expedition, acted with more promptness, energy and success. The Delawares and Shawnoes, the most hostile of the tribes, were reduced to entire submission, and the campaign closed with the prospect of permanent peace. That portion of the State of New York, embracing the Mohawk and Genesee Valleys, and the country lying between, was first known as the country of the Iroquois, the most warlike and powerful of the Indian nations —consisting originally of the Mohawks, Oneidas, Onondagas, Cayugas and Senecas, called the Five Nations, and after the admission of the Tuscaroras in 1715, the Six Nations. From the earliest known period, this celebrated confederacy, acting in its united capacity, had been the scourge of surrounding nations, far and near, almost exterminating many tribes, and compelling their remnants to seek refuge in the far West. The Hurons, inhabiting the country south of Lake Huron ; the Neutral Nation, on the north side of Lake Erie and the Niagara River; the Eries, on the south shore of Lake Erie; and the Andastes, in the lower valley of the Susquehanna, four powerful tribes, were utterly subdued and driven from their possessions by this powerful confederacy, between 1649 and 1675. The location of the Iroquois afforded great facilities, by means of water communication through the adjoining lakes and rivers, to push their hostile operations in every direction, and they were never at rest. The numerous powerful French expeditions sent out to humble and subdue these active and troublesome enemies, and the military posts established on their borders held them in check, but never conquered them ; and not until the campaign of 1779, with the army under Gen. Sullivan, were they made to feel that they must finally yield to a superior power. They have always exhibited the best attributes of savage superiority, but their power was chiefly due to their peculiar family and tribal organizations, and to close union and combined action in all their warlike operations.

The expedition under Gen. Sullivan in 1779, was sent out to chastise these hostile tribes, for their barbarous conduct at Wyoming and Cherry Valley, in the previous year, and prevent future incursions, by destroying their settlements, and driving them into Canada. It consisted of about 4,000 men—a force deemed sufficient to overcome all opposition, and to capture Fort Niagara, the favorite haunt of savages and tories, where, under the leadership of Brandt and Butler, their barbarous forays were organized. The army advanced by way of the Susquehanna and Tioga and Seneca Lake, to the Genesee River, defeating and driving the Indians from their villages, and utterly destroying all their dwellings and crops in the Genesee Valley, on both sides of Seneca and Cayuga Lakes, and in all that region. Although the Indians were severely chastised, the movements of Sullivan were so dilatory, that for lack of time, or other causes, he failed to reach Niagara, and the Fort remained to harbor our worst enemies, and exert an unfavorable influence over the Indians during the war, and to the period of its final surrender. Under British encouragement, the Indians continued the struggle for two or three years longer, but with the close of the Revolution all organized and open hostility ceased, and the way was opened for peaceful negotiation and permanent settlement. All that remain of these once proud and powerful Indian tribes are small remnants of the Mohawks on Grand River in Canada, of the Senecas at Allegany and Tonawanda, and of the Tuscaroras in the vicinity of the Falls.

In 1786, the conflicting claims of New York and Massachusetts to the territory lying west of Seneca Lake, were settled by commissioners on behalf of each State, awarding to New York the jurisdiction, and to Massachusetts the ownership of the soil, subject to the Indian title, excepting only a tract one mile in width along the Niagara River, then and since known as the New York Reservation.

With the exception of the tract four miles in width along the Niagara River, ceded by the treaty held with Sir Wm. Johnson in 1764, the Indians were the recognized owners and exclusive occupants of this whole territory.

In 1787, Oliver Phelps and Nathaniel Gorham purchased of the State of Massachusetts its entire interest in the territory referred to, and in 1788, held a treaty with the Indians, under which they obtained from them title to all that portion lying east of Genesee River, and also to a tract twelve by twenty-eight miles, lying west of that river. The latter was called the mill-seat tract, embracing the great water power at Genesee Falls. As an inducement to build a grist mill at that place—now

Rochester—the proprietors agreed to convey to Ebenezer Allen one hundred acres of land on the river. The mill was erected, and stood near the west end of the aqueduct. Augustus Porter was appointed to survey the land, taking the mill as the middle point up and down stream. The promised conveyance does not appear ever to have been made, but in a conveyance made by the same grantors of surrounding land, exception is made of the said one hundred acres, as conveyed to Allen, and this recognition was held to constitute a good title to, what is now, the richest district of the city of Rochester. Phelps and Gorham relinquished to the State of Massachusetts all the lands not purchased at the treaty referred to, and it was sold soon after to Robert Morris, the great financier of the Revolution. In 1797, the Indians ceded to Robert Morris the title to the residue of their lands lying west of Genesee River, with the exception of what were long known as their Reservations, surrounding their settlements, a small part of which they still retain.

The settlement of the lands acquired under the first treaty, commenced immediately, though under great difficulties and embarrassments. The country was, of course, without roads, and only accessible by tedious routes of difficult navigation—on the south by the Susquehanna and Tioga Rivers, and on the north by the Mohawk, Oneida Lake, and Seneca River. For many years the Indians were in an excitable state, and by no means friendly. They were still numerous, and undisputed owners of the country lying west of the Phelps and Gorham purchase. Stimulated by Canadian hatred and jealousy of American interests, they were regarded with fear by the early inhabitants, until after the signal defeat of the western tribes, by Gen. Wayne, in 1794.

Our country was just beginning to recover from the exhausting efforts of the Revolutionary war, and the people who left their eastern homes, were generally poor, with little else than strong arms, and brave hearts, to sustain them in the toils and hardships of the wilderness. Through great self-denial and patient suffering, they toiled on, until Indian alarms ceased, and Indian titles were extinguished. Improved health and comfort followed, and their arduous labors were finally crowned with broad possessions, and a generous competency. Before this happy condition was realized, by the later settlers, west of Genesee River, new sufferings awaited them, occasioned by the war of 1812. To these so far as relates to the frontier, we will refer in proper connection, after tracing the history of our more immediate neighborhood to that period.

The first occupation of lands in the vicinity of the Falls, was by the French, in connection with transportation across the portage, and the possession and defence of the landing places at both ends of it. They built as already stated Fort Little Niagara for the protection of the upper landing, and opened the road required for travel and transportation. This road first terminated a short distance above the rapids, but was changed, probably at the time Fort Little Niagara was built, to the landing place at that point. How large a space was cleared around the fort is not known, but doubtless enough to prevent a surprise, or give shelter to the Indians for an attack. Fort Schlosser and the large house referred to, were built by the English, and the house and adjoining lands occupied as early as 1763 by John Steadman. He cleared more land both at that place and along the high river bank opposite Goat Island, and set out an orchard of about 150 trees near his house, of which about a dozen are still standing. He also cleared about ten acres of the upper end of Goat Island, and put a number of goats there, from which fact the island derived its name. These goats all perished in the winter of 1780, memorable for its severity. No Indian name for this island is known. At an early day the proprietors gave it the beautiful and appropriate name of Iris Island, but the real goat was more acceptable to the public than the mythical goddess, and so the goats have it, and the original name is retained. It must have been an early Indian haunt, from the fact that a deposit of human bones was discovered upon it. Augustus Porter visited the island in 1806, and observed many names carved on the bark of beech trees, one of which with the date of 1769 was legible for many years afterwards. Deer were often seen on the island, and after the bridge was built one was driven into the rapids and made his way safely to the main shore, and another fled to the lower end of the island and boldly jumped over the precipice. There is ground for belief that the French built a sawmill at the Falls at an early day. If so, it fell into decay, and was rebuilt by the English. It is certain that Steadman was in possession of a sawmill situated at the head of the rapids in 1779.

Steadman himself, or by his agent, retained possession of the house and lands about Fort Schlosser, or Little Niagara as he still called it, and at the Falls, until removed by the lessees and purchasers of the State, by legal process. In 1801, Steadman applied to the Legislature of New York to confirm a pretended Indian title to a tract of about five thousand acres of land, bounded by Niagara River, Gill Creek, and a line extending east from Devil's Hole to said creek. He set forth in his petition, that at the Indian council with Sir Wm. Johnson held in 1764, the Indians executed a conveyance of the said tract to him ; and that the deed was deposited with Sir Wm. Johnson for safe keeping, and lost with his papers. The Legislature disregarded the claim, and a few years afterwards sold the land to other parties. In 1823, the heirs of Steadman brought a number of suits against the purchasers, and the test suit with the chief proprietor, was tried at Albany, and defended by the Attorney General, Samuel A. Talcott, and Judge Howell of Canandaigua. No evidence of title was shown, but on the contrary, it appeared that the treaty of 1764 by which the Indians ceded the land in question to the Crown, and the order in council prohibiting the purchase of Indian lands, except for the Government, were both of earlier date than the pretended conveyance to Steadman. It also appeared that John and Philip Steadman held for many years a lease from the British Government of the portage, conditioned for the exclusive right of transportation, and for the occupation of all the improved land about Schlosser, and a large tract of unimproved land adjoining, for the support of their teams and cattle. No other rights were ever granted by the British Government. It was shown that in 1779 John Steadman, for himself and brother, proposed to sell their cattle, horses, wagons and all other property on the premises, and to assign their lease of the portage and the lands about Schlosser. The proposition to assign the lease, and sell only the personal property, made by Steadman himself, showed that his title to the land was groundless.

No other erections or improvements were made, at or near the Falls, previous to 1805, and the Steadman Farm, as it is still called, was the only property occupied and improved in the vicinity at that time.

Although by the treaty of 1783, Great Britain recognized the great lakes as our northern boundary, yet under various pretexts, the forts at Oswego, Niagara and Detroit were not surrendered until 1796, after the ratification of Jay's treaty. Gen. Lincoln on his way westward to treat with the Indians in 1793, spent some time at Fort Niagara and at other points, on both sides of the river. Of Fort Schlosser he says, it was the place from which goods brought over the portage were formerly shipped, but being within the limits of the United States, the British had made a way on the west side of the river, though Fort Schlosser was still occupied by a British guard. He speaks well of Steadman's hospitality, and describes his house as standing on the bank of the river.

During the Revolution, British loyalists, or tories as they were more commonly called, fled from New York, Pennsylvania and New Jersey to Canada, and made permanent settlements along the river, and some of the baser sort took part in the bloody forays in the Mohawk and Susquehanna Valleys. Soon after Robert Morris purchased of Massachusetts the land lying west of Phelps & Gorham's purchase, he sold about three millions of acres to the Holland Land Company, with an agreement, afterwards fulfilled, to extinguish the Indian title. All the land titles in Niagara and several adjoining counties, are derived from that Company, except for lands included in the New York State Reservation.

In 1789, Ontario County included all that part of the State lying west of Seneca Lake. In 1802, Genesee included all west of Genesee River. In 1808, Niagara included all the territory in the counties of Niagara and Erie, and was divided as at present, in 1821. The officers of Niagara as first organized were Augustus Porter, First Judge; Asa Ransom, Sheriff; and Louis Le Coutoulx, Clerk; and after the set off of Erie County, Silas Hopkins, First Judge; Lothrop Cooke, Sheriff; and Oliver Grace, Clerk.

The only road leading through Niagara County to the river, previous to 1800, was known for many years, as the old Queenston road, leading from Batavia to Lewiston and Fort Niagara. There was then no wagon road, on the east side of the river, from the Falls to Buffalo. In 1801, the United States Government directed Gen. Moses Porter, then in command at Fort Niagara, to employ his troops in opening a road to connect Fort Niagara with a fort then contemplated to be built, on the high bluff at Black Rock. This road, still known as the Military road, was opened from the top of the mountain at Lewiston, by a course as direct as possible to Tonawanda, and thence onward two or three miles on a straight line, so far as to cut and burn the timber, for a road six rods in width. Few bridges were built, or other work done, to make it passable for teams. In consequence of a disagreement between the General Government and State authorities, the work was discontinued, and the road left in an

unfinished state, much to the injury of both parties, as was afterwards shown. If this road had been completed, it would greatly
have enhanced the value of the lands, then the property of the
State, and would have benefited the General Government in a
much higher degree, in facilitating transportation, and the movement of troops in the war of 1812.

In the year 1805, the State of New York first offered the lands
lying along the Niagara River for sale, and Augustus Porter
and Peter B. Porter, and Benjamin Barton and Joseph Annin,
jointly, purchased largely of the lands at Lewiston, Niagara
Falls, and Black Rock, and elsewhere along the river.

Augustus Porter first visited the Falls in 1795, and again in 1796,
on his way, chief of a company of surveyors and assistants, to
explore and lay out into townships, what has since been known as
the Western Reserve, at that time constituting a part of the great
Northwestern Territory. His first impressions of the natural
advantages of this locality, were decidedly favorable. Taking
into view its position, on what was then, and in all probability
would ever be, the great thoroughfare from east to west,
with the vast water power, that as settlement advanced, must
become very valuable, he could not but regard it as a point
worthy of attention whenever the lands should be opened for sale
and improvement. These views influenced him and his associates
in the purchases referred to, with reference to immediate occupation and improvement. In connection with his first visit in 1795,
he makes the following statement. That he with his friend
Judah Colt, made the journey on horseback, to Chippewa, U. C.,
and there took passage on a boat for Presque Isle (now Erie),
Pa. The British still held possession of the military posts of
Oswego, Niagara, Detroit and Mackinaw, and no American
vessels had then been built on the lakes. Of Buffalo he says,
the only residents at that time were Johnson, a British Indian
interpreter, whose house stood on the site of the present Mansion
House; Winnie, an Indian trader, and two other families. A

large part of the ground now occupied by the city was an un-
broken wilderness. Of the Western Reserve in 1796 he says,
not a white family resided within its limits. $\checkmark$ _o $\acute{o}$_i_i $\grave{z}$.

In 1805, Augustus Porter built a sawmill and blacksmith's
shop at Niagara Falls, preparatory to other improvements ; and
in 1806 removed his family from Canandaigua to the old
Steadman House near Fort Schlosser.

Benjamin Barton settled at Lewiston in 1807, and Peter B.
Porter at Black Rock in 1810.

Previous to 1805, little had been done to change the wild
character of the country.   Bears were common in the surrounding forests, and wolves so numerous as to prevent keeping sheep,
and so bold as frequently to approach within a short distance
of the Steadman house, and their hideous nightly howlings were
familiar sounds in all the region about the Falls.   Ducks and
geese abounded in the river, and deer and smaller animals were
very plentiful.   The Indians were quite numerous, and frequently seen in their canoes passing up and down the river,
fishing and hunting, and in small encampments along the shore.
Their costume consisted of a shirt, clout, leggins and mocas-
sins in summer, with the addition of a blanket coat and cap in
cool weather, and a knife and tomahawk stuck in a buckskin
belt.   The leading chiefs retained some importance in the esti-
mation of the old settlers, and were treated with kindness and
hospitality—always with good fare, and a bed of blankets and
buffalo skins.   I well remember Farmer's Brother, a noted Seneca chief, and his wife, being entertained at my father's house ;
and also a visit there, of three or four days, from Red Jacket
and his interpreter, and two young chiefs ; and when the visit
was ended, leaving in their canoes, well stocked with provisions,
and the indispensable bottle of whiskey.

Other characteristics of the wildness of this region, mentioned
by Charlevoix in 1721, continued for some years after settlement
commenced.   He says of his walk over the portage to the Falls,

that one cannot go ten paces without walking over an ant hill
or a rattlesnake. This was rather a strong statement, but a
hundred years later it expressed a good deal of truth. Ant
hills abounded until removed by improvements of the land, and
rattlesnakes were joint tenants, with a decided intention to retain
possession. Not many years before the war of 1812, Mr. Joshua
Fairbanks, who resided near the Whirlpool, killed in a single
day, in the spring, more than a hundred rattlesnakes, as they
ascended the bank of the river at that place, the only point at
which the ascent was possible.

For several years the land immediately about the Falls remained in a wild state; cedars and a thick undergrowth extended
along the margin of the river; stately oaks grew along the
lines of Buffalo and Main streets, some of them four and five
feet in diameter. Of these, but a single one remains, on the old
Porter Homestead, the last living memento of the epoch of La
Salle and Hennepin.

On the west side of the river, with the exception of a small
plot where Barnett's museum now stands, the whole flat from
Table Rock to the Clifton House was a swamp, covered chiefly
with cedars. Cedars also grew thickly on the declivities, below
the perpendicular banks, adding much to the general effect of the
scenery. The small islands in the rapids were the favorite
resort of eagles, building their nests in the lofty hemlocks and
cedars, and hovering over the wild waste of land and water,
secure from molestation.

For several years the descent to the ferry below the Falls was
down the rugged precipice, near the present inclined plane, with
the support only of bushes growing out of the crevices of the
rocks, and by means of logs placed at an inclination, with notches
cut for steps, answering the purpose of ladders. The river
crossing was made in common log canoes. At a later period, an
improvement was made on the primitive plan, by ladders connected and extending from top to bottom of the precipice, and

this was followed by a much more safe and convenient arrangement, substituting for ladders a square timber frame, enclosed and provided with easy winding steps. Larger and safer boats were also used for ferriage, and this, though apparently the most dangerous, has proved the safest ferry on the river.

In connection with the purchase of lands along the river, as before stated, and with a view to extended business operations, Augustus Porter and his associates obtained from the State a long lease of the landing places at Lewiston and Schlosser, with the exclusive privilege of transporting property across the portage. In aid of this business, they purchased and built a number of vessels on Lakes Erie and Ontario, and boats for the river; so that for a number of years, transportation over this route was largely controlled by the firm of Porter, Barton & Co. They transported Ononadaga salt in large quantities, and supplies for the military posts; also goods and furs for the extensive Indian trade of that period.

All the river transportation between Schlosser and Lake Erie was done by them in boats, and the transfer of freight made at Black Rock. Some years before the war, they built a pier and warehouse on Bird Island, where transfers were made in calm weather. Before the war of 1812, Porter, Barton & Co. were owners in whole or part of the following vessels on Lake Erie: sloops Erie and Niagara, and schooners Tracy, Amelia, Ranger, Mary and Contractor; and on Lake Ontario, schooners Niagara and Ontario.

Previous to 1796 all transportation on the lakes was by means of boats and British vessels.

William Savery, one of the deputation of the Society of Friends from Pennsylvania, associated with the United States Commissioners sent to treat with the Indians in 1793, in his journal says, the party went from Fort Niagara by way of Chippewa to Fort Erie, and there embarked on a British vessel furnished by Gov. Simcoe, for Sandusky. He states that at that time there were four British vessels on Lake Erie, and gives their names as follows : Chippewa, Detroit, Ottawa and Dunmore. There must have been at least as many on Lake Ontario. Upon the surrender by the British of the military posts of Oswego, Niagara and Detroit in 1796, settlement commenced along the American side of the lakes, and vessels were built as required, both on Lake Erie and Ontario. The British soon after built Forts George and Erie, and ceased to embarrass our free navigation of the lakes.

One of the first American vessels on Lake Ontario, was the schooner Jemima, built by Eli Granger at the mouth of Genesee River in 1797, and sold in 1798 to Augustus and Peter B. Porter, of which the original bill of sale is still preserved. From that time to 1812 a considerable number of vessels were built at Oswego and other ports. In 1808, the brig Oneida was built at Oswego for the United States service, and in 1809 the schooners Niagara and Ontario were built by Porter, Barton & Co., at Lewiston.

About 1800, the United States brig Adams was built at Detroit. In 1803, the schooner Contractor was built at Black Rock, and the sloop Niagara at Cayuga Creek. A number of vessels were built before the war, at Detroit, Erie, Black Rock, and elsewhere.

Most of the vessels fit for service at the commencement of the war, were purchased by the United States, and used as armed vessels or transports. After the war, the United States sold such vessels as were suitable for commercial purposes. In 1815, Porter, Barton & Co. and Townsend, Bronson & Co., of Oswego, united under the firm of Sill, Thompson & Co., and purchased and built several vessels, and resumed and continued the transportation business from Oswego to the upper lakes until 1821, when the lease of the portage expired. Other forwarding lines had been established, and the number of vessels increased rapidly.

The first American steamboat on Lake Ontario, called the

Ontario, was built in 1817. The first steamboat on Lake Erie, named from an Indian chief, Walk-in-the-Water, was built at Black Rock in 1818.

After the Erie Canal was opened in 1825, the lines of through transportation by way of Niagara River and the portage were discontinued.

In 1807, Porter, Barton & Co. built a grist mill at the Falls, and in order to obtain the force necessary to raise the frame, they were obliged to send to Fort Niagara for a detachment of soldiers.

In 1808, Augustus Porter built his dwelling house, which was destroyed in the war of 1812, and re-built on the same site, in 1818. He also built a rope-walk, in which he manufactured rigging from hemp raised on Genesee flats, for vessels on the lakes, both American and British. Other improvements soon followed; a tannery, a carding and clothes dressing establishment, several shops, a comfortable log tavern, and a number of small dwelling houses. A few settlements were made along the river, and on the military road. But the country was unhealthy, and the progress of improvement very slow. The following persons were householders in the village previous to 1812 : James Everingham, John W. Stoughton, Wm. Van Norman, Adoram Everingham, Joshua Fairchild, Ebenezer Hovey, Wm. Chapman, James Armstrong, John Sims, Jacob Hovey, Ezekiel Hill, Ralph Coffin, Ebenezer Brundage, and Oliver Udall. The following persons had purchased and settled on lands on the river and military roads: James Fields, Jacob Gilbert, Gad Pierce, Parkhurst Whitney, John and Abraham Wetmer, and Christian and Samuel Young,

The war of 1812 was a serious interruption to the progress of settlement and improvement here, and in all the surrounding country, and subjected the people to great sacrifices and sufferings. It was commenced without preparation, and for a long time attended with disaster and disgrace. The militia were called out by thousands, for defence and invasion, and in their

undisciplined condition, were unfit for either. Immediately
after the declaration of war, most of the families on the Niagara
frontier, removed to the interior, but generally returned to their
homes, and remained until the British and their Indian allies
invaded and laid waste our defenceless frontier.

In December, 1813, after the unjustifiable burning of New-
ark (now Niagara), by General McClure, and the disbanding
of the militia, the British with all their available force, crossed
the river, at night, at the Five Mile meadows, two miles below Lewiston, and surprised and captured Fort Niagara.
They then proceeded to Lewiston and the Falls, in their work
of destruction ; buildings were burned, and property plun-
dered, many unresisting persons killed, and others, only escaping with their lives, were reduced in many cases to ex-
treme want and suffering. At the Falls nothing was saved
except two or three small buildings, and the log tavern, all of
which were set on fire, but extinguished after the hasty departure
of the enemy. Shortly after, Buffalo and Black Rock had a
like visitation. No buildings were erected at the Falls until
1815. Though our people shared largely in the losses and dis-
couragements resulting from our numerous failures and defeats
during the first years of the war, they had afterwards occasions for
exultation in our successes. The disgraceful surrender of Gen.
Hull at Detroit, the disastrous result of the attempted invasion
of Canada at Queenston, and the destruction of their homes and
property, and the capture of Fort Niagara, were amply offset by
the success of Gen. Harrison at the West, the hard fought battles
on the Niagara Frontier, the defeat of the invading army at Platts-
burg, and the glorious victories of Perry and McDonough, resulting in the complete defeat and capture of both the British fleets.
These with the no less brilliant achievements of Hull, Bainbridge,
Decatur, Stewart, Porter and others, on the ocean, occasioned
universal rejoicing, and inspired strong confidence in our final
success. The battles of Niagara and Chippewa, the repulse of

the enemy in the assault on Fort Erie, and the gallant and successful sortie from that fort, by which the batteries of the enemy were destroyed and the siege raised, were among the bloodiest and most bravely contested battles of the war. Though no direct advantage was gained by the war, it had the important effect of teaching England thereafter to respect our rights by sea and land, as she had not previously done. *note 4,*

One battle scene of the war, ever to be remembered by the many spectators who witnessed it, was that of the successful landing of our army in Canada, and the destruction of Fort George.

The army designed for the service, under the command of Gen. Dearborn, had been encamped at Four Mile Creek, on the shore of Lake Ontario, for several days. Early on a bright and beautiful morning in June, 1813, a large number of boats having been provided, the order for embarcation was given, and as soon as completed, the flotilla, preceded by the fleet under Commodore Chauncey, moved slowly toward the point of attack. At the same time a heavy cannonade, with hot shot, was commenced from Fort Niagara and the batteries near Youngston, on the works at Fort George. The inner works were chiefly of heavy timber, in which the hot shot made a lodgment, and in a few hours the fort was demolished and burned. The vessels of the fleet, twelve or fifteen large and small, were drawn up in a semicircle around the point on which Fort Mississauga now stands, to cover the landing of the boats, and opened fire along the whole line, upon the British forces, posted on the bank and plain above. As the boats approached the shore, the enemy opened a well directed fire and made a spirited resistance for some time, but were finally routed, and our army marched directly to the fort, where our flag was soon displayed. The whole movement, including the destruction of the fort, the embarcation and landing of the army, the battle and the final rout, was witnessed by a large number of spectators from the banks of the lake and river and the plain around Niagara, and among them the narrator, then a lad of eleven years, in company with his father and elder brother. Shortly after the battle commenced, the batteries of the enemy, which had remained silent all the morning, opened upon the fleet and upon all our forces and defences. Shells burst frequently over the plain, and the fragments sometimes fell near groups of . spectators, scattering them, but not much diverting their attention from the interesting scene before them. Most of them remained to witness the destruction of the fort and the close of the battle.

Sixty years have passed since the close of our last contest with England, and we trust the scourge of war will never revisit these borders.

The early colonists of America, from the two great rival nations of England and France, long cherished their hereditary animosities, and our two wars with England taught us to look upon Canada in no friendly light. Separated by the great natural boundary of the lakes and the river St. Lawrence, our intercourse was for a long time, far from being free and friendly. But this wide and deep boundary—unlike the English Channel, the Alps or the Pyrenees, which must ever separate nations—no longer forms a barrier to free intercourse. The increase of international commerce through the lakes, and the numerous extensive lines of railroads, connected by the great bridges at Montreal, Niagara and Buffalo, have had a marked effect in removing all unfriendliness, and in harmonizing social and commercial relations between the two countries, so as to render it certain, that at no distant time, they will form one vast country, under the same institutions, extending from ocean to ocean, and from the Gulf of Mexico to the frozen regions of the North.

Looking at the condition of settlers west of Genesee River previous to the war of 1812, we find that a large portion of them were poor and in embarrassed circumstances, few of them having paid for their farms. A small class with more ample means, owners of large tracts of land, men of enterprise, and capital, were making valuable improvements, opening roads, building mills and vessels, and in various ways converting timber, and other products of the country, so as best to promote the progress of settlement and improvement. Between these two classes of men, there was then a distinction now wholly unknown. The large landholders and active capitalists, with the property qualification, then required of voters—which was finally abolished under the constitution adopted in 1821—exercised the chief political power. The great majority found full employment in the support of their families and improvement of their farms. But notwithstanding this inequality of outward circumstances, the most friendly and familiar relations existed between them. Few made any display of their more prosperous condition, and all maintained their self-respect and independence, and were unbounded in acts of generosity and kindness, and liberal in hospitality, according to their circumstances. Farmers were ever ready to aid one another in cases of sickness and misfortune, and to exchange labor of men and teams, in clearing land and gathering crops, in plowing and sowing; and even occasions of merry-making, called bees, were turned to profitable account. In primitive phrase the latch-string was always out, and all were made welcome around the broad hearth, and at the great wood fire and generously supplied table of the comfortable log dwelling. Such hospitality loses nothing by comparison, for where there is more of show and ceremony, there is likely to be less of sincerity and cordiality. Men of liberal means, not only reciprocated hospitalities with their immediate neighbors and friends, but extended like favors to strangers introduced by mutual friends. Taverns, or inns as they were then called, were not very commodious in that day, and gentlemen visiting the country usually brought with them letters of introduction, and were always kindly welcomed and entertained. Much was formerly claimed for Southern hospitality, but nowhere was the term more justly applied, than to the early settlers, of all conditions, in Western New York. The habits and customs of the people have greatly changed since that period, there is more wealth, and a great deal more display, but some of the best attributes of society have sadly degenerated. This is especially true in regard to the sympathies of a common brotherhood, which are nowhere found so strong, as among the inhabitants of a new country. The people were then plain, honest, frugal, industrious and hospitable—and without the overweening greed of money, characteristic of latter times— were contented and happy.

Taking another view of old times, there is no object more interesting than the old log school-house, and no character more worthy of remembrance than the country school-master. The model country school-house was built of logs, with the bark on, dovetailed at the corners, in size about 20 by 24 feet, a door on the front near the corner, a broad stone fire-place, with chimney of sticks plastered on the inside with clay, and two large stones for andirons, windows on three sides, six or eight feet long and two high, with writing tables arranged along the sides, and benches made of slabs, flat side up, with legs inserted in auger holes, so high as to accommodate the larger pupils, and keep the smaller ones in order, from the fear of falling off. The furniture was completed, by the addition of a birch of good proportions, resting on two pegs driven into a log, in a conspicuous place. Such a school-house was the first built at the Falls. It stood by the roadside, north of Ontario street, near the Hydraulic canal. The school-books in use were Noah Webster's Spelling Book, Dr. Jedediah Morse's Geography, Daboll's Arithmetic, Lindley Murray's English Grammar, and the English Reader—a selection from the best English authors—a list of school-books comparing favorably with any since introduced.

The teachers, at least some of them, had peculiar characteristics, soon understood by their pupils, and never forgotten. A few of these men, who were early employed in our village school, were fair samples of the order. The first was a bachelor, well

advanced, with a fair English education, and a smattering of
Latin. When he applied the birch, as he often did, with no
sparing hand, he did not fail to assure the victim that he would
thank him for his faithfulness to the end of his days. He was
an ardent Jeffersonian democrat, and fully adopted the sentiment,
and often repeated the democratic shibboleth of that day, *Vox
populi, vox Dei.* He had an infirmity of vision, as much con-
cealed and aided by the glasses he wore, a circumstance that
his pupils sometimes miscalculated to their sorrow. Like most
old bachelors, he had been disappointed in early love, and had
a habit of soliloquizing aloud on the subject. Of course he had
a tenderness for young lady pupils, that relieved in a degree,
the severity of his discipline, not only toward them, but toward
their offending brothers and favorites.

> " A man severe he was, and stern to view,
> I knew him well, and every truant knew—
> But passed is all his fame, and e'en the spot
> Where he once proudly triumphed, is forgot."

The second was a younger man, of genial temperament, who
added to his other qualifications, some taste and skill in drawing, which he turned to good account, in drawing men and
beasts and birds and fancy sketches, as rewards of merit. He
had a vein of humor, that sometimes displayed itself in original
and ridiculous forms of punishment. As for instance, in the
case of a miss of fourteen, where discipline seemed necessary,
instead of adopting the usual form of punishment, he called her
to his seat, and taking her on his knees, and gently holding her
with one hand, and with the other raising her club of carefully
braided hair, like a barber's pole, he gave her a smart trot with
a merry song and lively air, to the great mortification of the
young lady, and to the unbounded satisfaction and uproarious
delight of the whole school.

> He was a man of genius, ready wit,
> Fond of a joke, careless of where it hit.

The third was a man of decided amiability, and a painstaking and successful teacher. According to the custom of the day, he boarded around in the families of his patrons for a longer or shorter time, proportioned to the number of scholars in each. He had a fondness for music, that always made him an acceptable guest, and was a universal favorite, not only for his merits as a teacher, and for the mildness of his discipline, but for his marked attention to the mothers and elder sisters of his pupils; assisting the mothers in the care of the younger children, and aiding the daughters in more sociable and agreeable employments.

> He was a man, genial and kind and true,
> The mothers loved him, and the daughters too,
> And take him all in all, you seek in vain,
> To find a pedagogue like him again.

Such were our educational advantages. Our religious privileges, outside of family instruction, were so few and small as to be scarcely noticeable. For many years after settlement commenced, public religious services were of rare occurrence. The Methodist preachers who in post-revolutionary times, kept step with the advance of settlement westward, with scarcely less zeal, than was manifested by the early French Jesuits for the Indians, were uncultivated, but earnest and enterprising men, devoted to their arduous work. But the settlements were scattered far and wide, and the visits of these worthy men were few and far between, and probably not a dozen public religious services were held at the Falls previous to the close of the war, in 1815.

Returning to our narrative. At the conclusion of the war, most of the former inhabitants returned, the mills and dwellings were rebuilt; Parkhurst Whitney repaired and enlarged the old tavern, so as to make it a very comfortable resort for travelers; Samuel DeVeaux built a store and settled as a merchant in the village; transportation over the portage was resumed, and two or three years of peace repaired the ravages of war.

The year 1816 was a very unfavorable one throughout the

country. Monthly frosts throughout the whole season cut off the crops—provisions were dear and money scarce—but with a succession of more productive seasons, the country became comparatively prosperous.

In 1816, Augustus Porter purchased Goat Island of the State, and erected a bridge to connect it with the main shore, from a point near the head of the island. This bridge proved insufficient to resist the strong current and heavy masses of ice at that point, and was partially carried away in the first winter. In 1818, another bridge was constructed across the rapids, on the site of the present bridge, which has proved to be a secure position. For the old bridge of wood, the present bridge of iron was substituted in 1856. A cloth-dressing and wool-carding establishment was erected by James Ballard, in 1816, and soon after enlarged, by D. & S. Chapman, for the manufacture of woolen cloth and satinet. In 1819–20, Parkhurst Whitney built a large addition to his tavern, giving it the name of Eagle Tavern. In 1821, a forge, rolling mill and a nail factory were built and carried on by Bolls & Gay.

In 1822, Augustus Porter built a large flouring mill, now owned by Wetmer Brothers. In 1823, a paper mill was built by Jesse Symonds, near Goat Island bridge. In 1826, the upper race was extended, and Ira Cook, Wm. G. Tuttle, Chapin & Swallow, and others, erected works of different kinds upon it. In 1826, a large paper mill was built on Bath Island by Porter & Clark, aftewards purchased and enlarged by L. C. Woodruff.

In 1825, the Erie Canal was completed, and a large water-power was drawn from it, at Lockport and elsewhere, which had the effect to check improvement here, and transfer it to the line of the canal, consequently little addition was made to population or business at the place for several years.

In 1836, a year of extravagant speculation throughout the country, Benjamin Rathbun, a well-known hotel-keeper, builder, banker, and speculator in real estate, made large contracts for

the purchase of real estate in this village and vicinity. He
built a large addition to the Eagle Tavern and laid the
foundation for a very extensive hotel on the square now occupied by the International Hotel. The village plan was greatly
enlarged, and he commenced a sale of village lots at auction,
with good prospects of success, in the midst of which, the bub-
ble burst, by his sudden and unexpected failure, with injurious
effect to our village, and with still greater loss to many of his
friends in Buffalo, the seat of his most extensive operations.

In December, 1837, during the Canadian rebellion, an affair
occurred at what is known as the Gill Creek Landing, about two
miles above the Falls, of some historical interest, known as the
" Caroline affair." A small American steamer, called the Caroline, had been employed for several days in transporting men
and supplies in connection with a large military force, composed
chiefly of American citizens, occupying Navy Island, and
threatening the invasion of Canada. It being well known that
the steamer was moored at night at the dock on the American
shore, an expedition conducted by Alexander McLeod, left
Chippewa in the night, and reaching the American shore unob-
served, captured the steamer, dispersing the crew and leaving
one man on the dock dead. The steamer was towed into the
river, set on fire, and left to drift over the Falls. This high-
handed act excited great popular indignation, and for a time
seriously threatened the peace of the two countries. Both parties were in the wrong, and as usual in such cases, both were
glad to settle the matter fairly and restore friendly relations.

In 1836, railroads were built and put in operation between
Buffalo and Lockport and Niagara Falls, and though slightly
built, answered a very good purpose, for the light traffic and
travel of that period, and served greatly to relieve our village in
the general reaction of 1836, and the embarrassments of two or
three years afterwards. In 1845, an inclined plane, with cars
operated by water power, was substituted for the old mode of

descending the river bank, by winding steps at the ferry. In 1852, the railroad to Lockport was extended to Rochester, and in 1853, the Canandaigua & Niagara Falls Railroad, by way of Batavia, was completed.

The first suspension bridge across Niagara River, intended only as temporary work, from which to construct the permanent bridge, was erected by Charles Elliott in 1848. The great railroad bridge was completed in 1855, on the plans and under the personal superintendence of John A. Robling, who shortly before his death, made the plans and commenced the work of the much greater suspension bridge between New York and Brooklyn. The suspension bridge for carriage travel, at Lewiston, was built in 1851, and destroyed in a severe gale a few years after. The suspension bridge near the Falls, of a similar kind, was opened for travel in 1869. The railroad iron arch bridge at Black Rock was completed in 1874.

A small steamboat was built in 1848, for the river below the Falls, and was succeeded by a larger and stronger one in 1854. In 1861, the latter proving unprofitable, was safely navigated through the rapids to Lewiston. A similar feat, though unattended with risk to human life, was performed in the rapids above the Falls in 1829, as a matter of experiment and curiosity. An old schooner was set adrift in the middle of the river above the rapids, and though badly broken, and completely water-logged in her passage through the rapids, yet following the deep current to the center of the horse-shoe, though drawing from twelve to fifteen feet water, passed over the Falls, apparently without touching bottom, thus showing the depth of water at that point.

The Cataract House was first built by David Chapman, in 1824, and enlarged from time to time by Parkhurst Whitney & Sons. The International Hotel, built by B. F. Childs in 1853, enlarged by J. T. Bush, and occupying the site of the primitive log tavern, ranks with the Cataract, among the largest and best hotels in the country. The Niagara House and Spencer House here, and the Monteagle Hotel at Suspension Bridge, are of more recent date, and are all hotels of high character and large capacity.

The Hydraulic Canal, which extends from deep water, above the rapids, to the high bank below the Falls, is of much importance to the convenient use of our great water-power. It effectually obviates all inconvenience from ice, and affords abundant supply of water, with a fall, practically unlimited. Augustus Porter, who owned the land through which this canal passes, early saw its importance, and for many years before his death, made the most liberal offers to capitalists to undertake the work, involving a greater expense than his own means would afford. His heirs believing in his estimate of the importance of the work, finally succeeded in securing the means necessary for the purpose, by a free gift of the water-power and about seventy acres of land, lying in the village, adjoining the lower end of the canal. The canal was completed several years ago, but for various reasons only recently improved. In 1874, two of our enterprising business men purchased one of the mill seat lots, and erected upon it a large flouring mill, which was completed about the first of February, 1875, and was in constant operation, through the coldest part of that extremely cold winter, without the slightest interruption from ice, or any other cause. This mill, valuable in itself, has an additional value, in demonstrating the perfection of our water power, and will doubtless lead to its extended use for other manufacturing establishments, greatly for the benefit of our village, and affords a gratifying proof of the correct judgment and liberal policy of the original proprietors.

The first common school was opened in this town in 1807, and good schools have been ever since maintained. In 1851 and 1854, two large stone school-houses, of three stories each, were erected in the village. In 1852, an academy was built, by one of the early proprietors, and conducted with much success, as a classical school for several years. The building is still occupied for educational purposes on another plan. Our common schools were made free in 1855. Samuel DeVeaux, an early settler in the village, who died in 1854, made a large bequest for the establishment of an institution, for the support and education of orphan boys. The trust was faithfully and successfully executed, and the institution known as DeVeaux College, located near Suspension Bridge, has been for several years in successful operation.

Church Societies were formed in this town in the following order : Methodist in 1815, Presbyterian in 1824, Episcopal in 1830, Baptist in 1848, Catholic in 1848. Public religious services were held for several years in the village school-house. A small union church was built and occupied by the Methodists, Episcopalians and other denominations, about 1828. The Presbyterians maintained regular services in the school-house from 1824 to 1831, when they built a church on the south-east corner of Fall and First streets. The Episcopal church on First street was built in 1847. The Presbyterians erected their present stone church on First street in 1849, and sold their old church to the Methodists. The Methodists built their stone church on First street in 1871. The Catholics built their stone church on Fourth street in 1849, afterwards greatly enlarged it, and built the new front, with tower and spire, in 1874. The Episcopalians completed the walls and tower of their new stone church on Union street in 1873-4. The Congregational church at Suspension Bridge was organized in 1855, and the church built in 1858; the Episcopal church in 1859, and the church built in 1866. Other smaller churches have been formed at that place within a few years.

Weekly newspapers have been published at the Falls as follows: *Iris of Niagara*, by Geo. H. Hackstaff from 1847 to 1854; *Niagara Falls Times*, by Wm. E. Tunis from 1855 to 1857; *Niagara Falls Gazette*, by Pool & Sleeper from 1854 to 1864, and by Wm. Pool since 1864. At Suspension Bridge sev-

eral papers, under different names, have been published since
1855. The *Suspension Bridge Journal* was established in 1870.

Gas works were built at the Falls in 1860, by which gas is supplied to both villages, and conveyed to Canada by pipes laid on
the suspension bridge. In addition to the buildings already
named, our village contains shops for various purposes, operated
by water power; and all the trades and occupations common to
ordinary towns. A large number of mechanics are employed in
the extensive building and repairing shops of the New York
Central Railroad Company. We have dry goods, grocery and
provision, hardware, boot and shoe, druggist, and jewelry stores,
and a large number of fancy and variety stores, supplied with rare
and beautiful goods, sold in large quantities to visitors at the
Falls.

A number of artists are constantly employed in the manufacture of photographic views of the Falls, for which they find
ready sale, both at home and abroad. We have, also, ministers,
lawyers, doctors, and teachers, in due proportion. Our streets
are lined with shade trees, and lighted with gas, and carriages
for the convenience of visitors are numerous, and kept in the
best possible condition of neatness and order.

The population of Niagara Falls taken in 1875 was about
3,500, and that of the town, 6,876.

Our village possesses great advantages, both natural and
artificial, in its healthful atmosphere, its unequaled water-
power, its extended railroad connections, its magnificent bridges
and hotels, and in the world-wide fame of the great Cataract.
These advantages insure a certain and steady, if not rapid
growth, and render it more and more a great center of resort,
from all parts of our country and the world. That it did not
increase as rapidly as the early settlers expected, was owing to
causes not at first foreseen, but now well understood. Situated
on the great natural channel of communication between the
lakes and the ocean, it was reasonable to expect, that with the

improvement of the country, near and remote, the vast water power, so favorably situated, would be rapidly improved, with the usual result of labor and enterprise. But before the village had recovered from the effects of the war; and while the surrounding country, suffering from other embarrassments, was making slow progress in improvement, at the early period of 1825, the Erie Canal was opened in its full extent. The immediate effect was, to divert the business of transportation from the old channel, and attract all enterprise and capital to the numerous villages growing up on the canal. Another injurious effect of the canal on this locality, though beneficial to the new villages, was the large water power it afforded, at points where little or none had previously existed—at Black Rock, Lockport, Medina, and other towns west of Rochester; adding greatly to their growth, and proportionably diminishing ours.

There is one point of view of peculiar interest connected with this locality. Considering the vast and uniform flow of water, with a fall of more than three hundred feet, in a distance of seven miles, we should naturally expect great changes to be constantly and rapidly going on; and we may well credit some of the plausible and interesting theories of geologists, based upon a cause so powerful, operating through an unlimited period. Changes have occurred, probably at no very remote period, in the bed of the river, opposite and above Goat Island, with little or no disturbance of the rock formation. Goat Island has undoubtedly been much larger than at present, covering the extensive shoal lying above it, and has been gradually reduced to its present dimensions, by the rapid current along its sides; an operation that would have swept away the whole island, but for the fact, that the part remaining, is based on a rock formation, rising at the head above the level of the river, and is shielded on both sides, by a number of small islands or masses of rocks, securing it against the action of water and ice—outposts and guards against future encroachment. This theory is well illustrated by a similar operation, within the recollection of the narrator. Little more than fifty years ago, there was a small island, called Gull Island, situated near the middle of the west channel, and opposite about the center of Goat Island, thirty or forty rods long and two or three rods wide, rising so much above the level of the river, as to sustain a considerable growth of shrubs and rushes. By some change in the current, caused probably by an unusual rise of water, it was gradually worn away, and after a few years, entirely disappeared.

Great changes in the Falls have taken place since Hennepin's view was taken. Within the recollection of many persons still residing here, rocks have fallen in immense masses, materially changing the contour of the Falls. A large portion of Table Rock fell in 1818. Another fall occurred in the bed of the river, extending several hundred feet from Table Rock into the channel, in 18e8. Again another portion of Table Rock fell in 1850; and in 1852, a large mass fell near Goat Island, westward. Smaller portions of rock are frequently falling, in both channels of the river, of which no particular note is taken.

Hereafter, changes that occur may be more definitely described. In 1842, James Hall and E. M. Blackwell made a careful trigonometrical survey of the Falls and vicinity, planting permanent stone monuments, and inserting copper bolts in the rocks at prominent points, on both sides of the river, and on Goat Island. This survey, made by authority of the State, with a map showing all the stations and bearings, is published in the Natural History of the State of New York. A re-survey from the same points, at any future time, will show, by comparison with the survey of 1842, any changes that may have taken place. Future changes in the configuration of the Falls, may also be shown hereafter, by comparison with photographic views, taken in great perfection, for several years past, from every accessible point, above and below the Falls.

To us, who have lived for many years within sight and hear-

ing of the great Cataract, Niagara is a household word, associated with our earliest and happiest recollections. Long familiar-
ity has in no degree lessened its grandeur or moral power.
There is an enchantment in the scene, strongly felt by persons
who have lived long within its influence, scarcely to be found
elsewhere. Nowhere is the great law of change more impres-
sively taught. Generation succeeds generation, and all the
works of human skill and labor perish—here we have strikingly
illustrated, the fact, that change, slow but sure and unmistaka-
ble, is passing upon the very rocks, and that they too are yield-
ing to the all subduing power of natural forces.

One point of deepest interest, still claims our special notice.
It will readily occur to all, that we refer to our pleasant rural
cemetery, situated on the high ground north of the village
limits, where a numerous company are already gathered, and
where many of us expect to find our final resting-place. Here
rest the pioneers of the wilderness, their toils all ended, and a
rich inheritance transmitted their children. Here too repose the
martyrs of the great rebellion, their battles fought, and their
cause victorious. And side by side with these, are loving
friends and dearest kindred, over whose graves we linger in
fond remembrances of the past, and bright hopes of the future.
Even in that retired spot, the associations of the Cataract meet
us. As we follow our friends, one after another, to their last
resting-place, where all else is quiet, the roar of the Cataract
falls heavily on our ears, suggesting the sublime thought, that
this *Voice of many Waters* will be their ceaseless requiem, until
the *Trump* of the *Resurrection*, rising above all earthly sounds,
shall hush it in everlasting silence.

This centenary year of our national life, marks a period half
as long as our whole local history.

Two hundred years ago, the light of civilization had not
dawned on this benighted region. A howling wilderness spread
out on every side, where wild beasts roamed in their native fe-

rocity, and tribes of savage men, more cruel still, waged un-
ceasing wars of extermination. So it had been for ages, and
so it would have been for ages to come, but for the introduction of Christian Civilization.

La Salle and his brave followers laid the foundation for a new
history. The fort at Niagara, and the Griffin—the pioneer of
the upper lakes—foretold conquest and discovery, and change
of race, slow but certain.

The ambition and jealousy of rival nations waged long and
bloody wars for supremacy, and the conquering nation had still
to settle the question of final sovereignty within itself. Two
wars with England—long since closed—were the last obstacles in
the way of progress and improvement, and left the kindred
nations to exercise rivalry, only in the arts of peace.

When we review our eventful history, and note the changes of
the last half century, where shall we find, in our whole broad
land, a locality so full of interest and promise? If our Union
and free institutions are maintained, and the good Providence of
God continues to protect and prosper our nation in the future,
as in the past, Niagara has a pledge of growth and greatness, as
stable as her rocks, and abundant as her flowing waters.

NOTES.

Note 1.—Captain Puchot, commandant at Fort Niagara from 1756 to the surrender in 1759, in his Memoir of the French War, from 1755 to '60, fully describes Niagara River, the Falls, the Rapids at Black Rock, and the Islands; also the situation and character of the fortifications at Fort Niagara; the portage and the landing places, and Fort Little Niagara.

There was a wagon road from Fort Niagara to the lower portage landing (Lewiston), used chiefly in winter when the navigation was obstructed by ice. The portage road, passing through woods and wet land, was very bad; that part of it extending from the landing to the top of the mountain, was circuitous and poorly constructed, and the ascent very difficult. A very steep pathway, leading directly from the river to the summit, was used by travelers and pack-carriers. On the lower bank were three buildings, and on the upper one, used as warehouses for goods in transit. There were also warehouses at Fort Little Niagara for storage of public property, and the goods of Indian traders. The stone used at Fort Niagara was brought from the mountain, lime from Frontenac, and timber from the banks of the Chenondac—Chippewa Creek.

Note 2.—The tradition referred to of French vessels burned near Grand Island, Capt. Puchot indirectly contradicts, when he says, "Lake Erie had not been explored by any person capable of giving an accurate description of it, and was only navigated with bark canoes and batteaux." And again he says, "It would have been well to have built a small vessel, with which, from May to September, when the navigation is always good, to sound and reconnoiter all the shelters around Lake Erie, so as to build vessels proper for the navigation, which would save great labor and expense."

Note 3.—The Western Reserve included the territory lying between the 41st degree of latitude, and Lake Erie; and the west line of Pennsylvania, and a meridian line drawn 120 miles west of said line. It had never been surveyed, but was supposed to contain about 3½ millions of acres, and the Connecticut Land Company purchased on that estimate. But when Augustus Porter had completed the traverse of the lake shore, it was found to extend further south than had been supposed, so as not to include the quantity named; and to cut off entirely a surplus, that had been expected, by a speculative association, called the Excess Company. So much dissatisfaction was expressed by the latter company with Mr. Porter's estimate, that the Professor of Mathematics from Yale College was employed to review his calculations. Much to the satisfaction of Mr. Porter, and to the disappointment of the Excess Company, his calculations were found correct, and were approved and adopted.

Note 4.—Before the war of 1812, England had given repeated causes of offence; in withholding the military posts, and encouraging the hostility of the Indians; in embarrassing our commerce, and impressing our seamen; doubtless in the belief, that our government could not survive a war; otherwise she would not have provoked it, while so deeply involved in the great European struggle. Since that war, no Order in Council has embarrassed our commerce, and no American sailor has been impressed; our boundaries have been amicably and justly settled, and no cause of offence given, to the time of the great Rebellion; and the wrongs then allowed, have been frankly acknowledged, and our claims honestly paid.